A CENTURY
OF STORIES
NEW HANOVER COUNTY PUBLIC LIBRARY
1906-2006

INDIAN OCEAN

Jen Green

WORLD ALMANAC® LIBRARY

Please visit our web site at: www.worldalmanaclibrary.com
For a free color catalog describing World Almanac® Library's list of
high-quality books and multimedia programs, call 1-800-848-2928 (USA)
or 1-800-387-3178 (Canada). World Almanac® Library's fax: (414) 332-3567.

Library of Congress Cataloging-in-Publication Data

Green, Jen.
    Indian Ocean / Jen Green.
        p. cm. — (Oceans and seas)
    Includes bibliographical references and index.
    ISBN 0-8368-6273-2 (lib. bdg.)
    ISBN 0-8368-6281-3 (softcover)
    1. Indian Ocean—Juvenile literature. 1. Title.
    GC721.G74 2006
    551.46'15—dc22   2005054136

First published in 2006 by
World Almanac® Library
A Member of the WRC Media Family of Companies
330 West Olive Street, Suite 100
Milwaukee, WI 53212 USA

Copyright © 2006 by World Almanac® Library.

Produced by Discovery Books
Editor: Sabrina Crewe
Designer and page production: Sabine Beaupré
Photo researcher: Sabrina Crewe
Maps and diagrams: Stefan Chabluk
Geographical consultant: Keith Lye
World Almanac® Library editorial direction: Valerie Weber
World Almanac® Library editor: Gini Holland
World Almanac® Library art direction: Tammy West
World Almanac® Library graphic design: Charlie Dahl
World Almanac® Library production: Jessica Morris and Robert Kraus

Picture credits: Corbis: cover, pp. 6, 14, 27, 29, 33, 34, 37, 39 (both), 41; FLPA: pp. 12
(both), 20, 22 (top), 23, 24 (top), 25 (left), 30 (bottom), 31, 32, 38 (bottom), 40, 42, 43;
Getty Images: pp. 8, 11 (both), 13, 19 (both), 28, 30 (top), 38 (top); NASA: p. 18; NOAA:
pp. 21, 24 (left and bottom), 25 (right), 35; NOAA/NGDC: title page.

Printed in the United States of America

1 2 3 4 5 6 7 8 9 10 09 08 07 06

CONTENTS

Front cover: *Much of the Indian Ocean is in the world's tropical and subtropical regions, where the climate is warm and wet. Palm trees and other lush vegitation grow along the ocean's shores.*

Title page: *This computer-generated image of Earth was based on land and ocean measurements made by the U.S. National Geophysical Data Center. This view shows the Indian Ocean, with the continents bordering it visible as yellow, green, and pale orange areas. The image also shows ridges and plateaus in the ocean itself. The dark orange area at the bottom is the continent of Antarctica.*

Words that appear in the glossary are printed in **boldface** the first time they occur in text.

The Indian Ocean is the third largest ocean in the world. It covers about 26.5 million square miles (68.6 million square kilometers), making it more than five times the size of the United States.

Boundaries of the Indian Ocean

The Indian Ocean is bounded by eastern Africa and the Arabian **Peninsula** to the west. Southern Asia lies to the north, while Indonesia and Australia are in the east. The Southern Ocean lies to the south. The Indian Ocean has a few large islands, including Sumatra, Java, and Madagascar. There are several seas and other bodies of water that are within the Indian Ocean's boundaries—these include the Red Sea and Persian **Gulf**; the Arabian Sea and the Gulfs of Aden and Oman; and the Andaman Sea and the Bay of Bengal.

In the east, the Indian Ocean includes the Strait of Malacca and the Java, Flores, Savu, and Timor Seas. Beyond those waters lies the Pacific Ocean. The Indian Ocean also meets the Pacific at Tasmania, south of Australia. In the southwest, the Indian Ocean merges with the Atlantic at the southern tip of Africa.

Astonishing Islands

"Every one must be struck with astonishment, when he first beholds one of these vast rings of coral-rock . . . here and there surmounted by a low verdant island with dazzling white shores, bathed on the outside by the foaming breakers of the ocean, and on the inside surrounding a calm expanse of water. . . ."

Naturalist Charles Darwin, describing coral islands he saw in the Indian Ocean, Coral Reefs, *1842*

A Stormy Climate

The Indian Ocean is known for its **currents** that reverse direction with the seasons because of changing winds called monsoons. These variable winds have a major influence on climate and farming, especially in the north. Fierce storms and huge floods often strike the region.

Resources

The Indian Ocean has been important for trade and shipping since ancient times. It has acted as a highway for peoples and cultures. Today, it is known for its rich **mineral** resources, especially oil in the Persian Gulf.

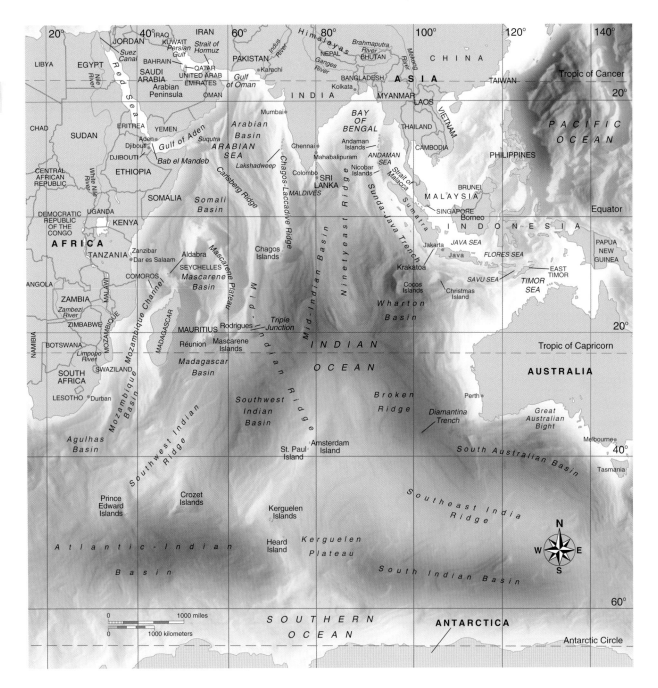

This map shows the Indian Ocean, its major islands and underwater features, and the landmasses that border it.

Indian Ocean Key Facts

Surface area: 26,469,472 square miles (68,556,000 sq km)

Coastline: 41,339 miles (66,526 kilometers)

Average depth: 13,002 feet (3,963 meters)

Deepest known points: 24,500–25,344 feet (7,450–7,725 m) in the Sunda-Java
Trench and 24,250–26,400 (7,390–8,050 m) in the Diamantina Trench

CHAPTER ONE

PHYSICAL FEATURES

Below the surface of the Indian Ocean, deep basins and trenches are separated by towering mountains, often linked in long chains. About fifty years ago, scientists realized that all of these features were formed by movements of the huge slabs of rock, called tectonic plates, which make up Earth's outer layers. These movements and other factors ensure that the Indian Ocean is still changing today.

Plate Movement

Several tectonic plates lie below the Indian Ocean. Running slightly west of the ocean's center, a long undersea **ridge**—the Mid-Indian Ridge—marks a boundary between two plates that are slowly pulling apart. There, the ocean floor is gradually getting wider as **magma** wells up to fill the gap, pushing the older rock on either side out toward the edges of the ocean. At these edges, plates may collide with other plates. In the northeast, off the Indonesian islands of Java and Sumatra, the large Indian and Australian Plates are colliding with the small Burma and Sunda Plates to the east. The dense rock of the large plates slides below the smaller, lighter plates, forming deep trenches, such as the Sunda-Java Trench. Because of these movements, earthquakes are common around Indonesia.

Bali is an island at the southern end of the Sunda-Java Trench. In January 2004, an earthquake there caused severe damage to houses and other buildings.

Earth's outer layers are made up of a number of vast, rigid sections called tectonic plates—seven major ones and up to twelve smaller ones. Fitting together like pieces of a jigsaw puzzle, the plates underlie oceans and dry land. The plates drift across Earth's surface, floating on a lower, molten layer of the **mantle** like chunks of bread on a thick, bubbling soup. As they drift, tectonic plates can push together, grind past one another, or pull apart.

About 250 million years ago, Earth's landmasses were united in a single "super-continent" named Pangaea, which was surrounded by a vast ocean now known as Panthalassa. About 200 million years ago, because of **continental drift** caused by plate movement, a great bay—the Tethys Sea—opened up in the center of Pangaea and split it in half. The northern landmass—named Laurasia—included North America, Greenland, Europe, and Asia, while the southern half—Gondwanaland—included South America, Africa, India, Australia, and Antarctica. About 130 million years ago, the plate bearing India slowly separated from Antarctica and drifted north at the rate of 2–4 inches (5–10 centimeters) a year. India collided with the rest of Asia about 45 million years ago. The rocks of the collision zone buckled upward to form the mighty Himalaya mountains and several ridges that now lie on the bed of the Indian Ocean. The plate bearing Africa, meanwhile, drifted west, and Australia separated from Antarctica. Over millions of years, the continents and oceans took their present positions (shown above, with the major tectonic plates), and they continue to shift today. The Indian Ocean had reached its present shape by about 35 million years ago.

Volcanoes and Earthquakes

In 1883, the Krakatoa volcano on a tiny island in Indonesia exploded in a violent eruption. The explosion caused the loudest bang ever recorded, which was heard 3,000 miles (4,800 km) away in Australia. The upheaval raised huge **tsunamis** that swept across the Indian Ocean, drowning thirty-six thousand people on islands and coasts.

On December 26, 2004, a massive earthquake rocked the seabed off Aceh Province in Sumatra, Indonesia. Rating a huge 9.0–9.2 on the **Richter Scale**, this was the world's worst quake for forty years. Rocks along a line of weakness stretching 600 miles (965 km) had shifted sideways and downward by several feet. The earthquake, and the shock waves that followed, sent tsunamis traveling outward at hundreds of miles per hour, with deadly results. Another massive earthquake, just 100 miles (160 km) south along the Sumatra coast and measuring 8.7, followed in March 2005.

The Mid-Indian Ridge

One of the main features of the Indian Ocean bed is a series of undersea ridges shaped like a letter "Y" turned on its head. This Y-shaped ridge system includes the Carlsberg Ridge, the Mid-Indian Ridge, and the Southwest Indian Ridge. New rock is forming at several sites along these ridges, which are marked by deep cracks caused by undersea earthquakes.

Other Ridges

The ocean floor is also changing at several other sites in the region, including in the center of the Red Sea, which is widening by 0.5 in (1.27 cm) a year. The Indian Ocean has other ridges, called aseismic

Ash rises from Anak Krakatoa, a new volcanic peak that has formed in the area occupied by Krakatoa. The original volcano was blown to pieces in the eruption.

In 1977, scientists exploring the Pacific Ocean depths in **submersibles** made an amazing discovery. They found extraordinary rock chimneys belching clouds of scalding water, black with the minerals sulfur and iron. These hydrothermal vents, also called "black smokers," are now thought to occur in volcanically active regions in many parts of the oceans. In 2000–2001, U.S. and Japanese scientists located several hydrothermal vents in the Indian Ocean on the Mid-Indian Ridge at and around Triple Junction, where the African, Australian, and Antarctic plates intersect. At hydrothermal vents, ocean water entering cracks in the crust is heated and mixed with newly erupted minerals to gush out again in dark clouds of hot water. The minerals settle and build up around the vents to form chimneys. They also seep out into the ocean, adding to the water's salt levels. "White smokers" have also been found—these vents spew slightly cooler water containing white minerals.

ridges, where there is little or no volcanic activity. Aseismic ridges include the Ninetyeast Ridge, which runs south from the Bay of Bengal.

Plateaus and Trenches

As well as steep ridges, the floor of the Indian Ocean has high, flat areas called plateaus, such as the Mascarene and Kerguelen Plateaus. Ridges and plateaus separate the ocean into deep, flat-bottomed basins, including the Mid-Indian, Wharton, and South Australian Basins.

Deep trenches form in **subduction zones** where tectonic plates are colliding

The deep Sunda-Java Trench marks the subduction zone where plate movement caused the huge earthquake of December 26, 2004. This map shows the areas that were most affected by the earthquake and subsequent tsunamis. Somalia and the Seychelles, not shown here, were also struck by tsunamis.

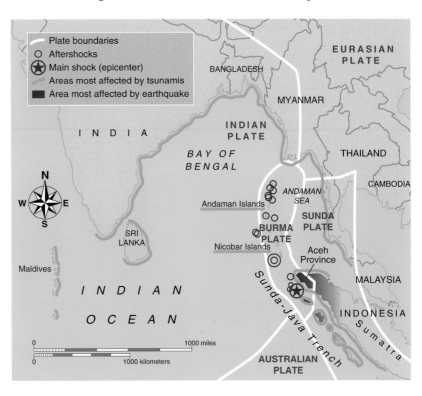

The Southern Ocean

The most southern waters of the Indian Ocean meet those of the Southern Ocean. The Indian Ocean used to include part of the Southern Ocean. In 2000, however, the Southern Ocean was officially declared a separate ocean. The Southern Ocean stretches across 7,848,255 square miles (20,327,000 sq km) of Earth's most southern region, surrounding the icy continent of Antarctica. Much of the ocean is covered by ice in winter. With its strong winds and freezing temperatures, the Southern Ocean is inhospitable to human settlement, but some animals also found in the Indian Ocean, including species of penguins and seals, live there.

beneath the ocean. The deepest points discovered so far in the Indian Ocean are in the Sunda-Java Trench and in the Diamantina Trench off the coast of Perth, Australia.

Plains and Shelves

Vast expanses of the Indian Ocean bed are occupied by deep areas called abyssal plains. A thick layer of **sediment** that was washed out to sea from land covers these plains. Close to shore, the wide, flat ledges of continental shelves edge landmasses bordering the ocean. There, the waters are about 500 feet (152 m) deep. The continental shelves of the Indian Ocean are fairly narrow compared to those of other oceans—mostly about 75 miles (120 km) wide, extending to 190 miles (300 km) off eastern India and northwest Australia. Where rivers enter the ocean, deep canyons cut into the shelves. The rivers carry sediment far out to sea to form vast **submarine fans** on the ocean floor. The Bengal Fan, created by the Brahmaputra and Ganges Rivers, is the world's largest such fan. It covers the entire floor of the Bay of Bengal.

Islands of the Indian Ocean

In addition to large islands, such as Madagascar and Sri Lanka, there are thousands of smaller islands in the

This diagram shows some of the features that form on Earth's ocean floors.

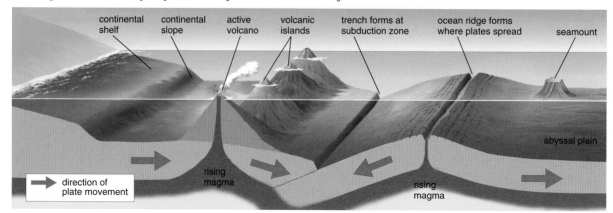

continental shelf · continental slope · active volcano · volcanic islands · trench forms at subduction zone · ocean ridge forms where plates spread · seamount · abyssal plain · rising magma · rising magma · direction of plate movement

Indian Ocean, often found in groups. The islands can be divided into three main types that formed in different ways: continental islands, oceanic islands, and coral atolls.

Continental islands include Sri Lanka and Madagascar and are formed from rocks similar to those on nearby continents. These fragments of land were once part of neighboring continents, but they became separated by tectonic plate movement or by rising ocean levels. Water levels in all oceans have been rising slowly for the last twenty thousand years.

Oceanic islands usually lie farther out to sea than continental islands. The Andaman and Nicobar Islands in the Bay of Bengal, formed by volcanic eruption, are located near subduction zones. They are the tops of volcanic peaks that have risen from the ocean bed. Other groups of oceanic islands, such as those of Comoros near Madagascar, form in zones called **hot spots**. In these areas, a plume of magma breaks through a weak spot in

Madagascar (above), a continental island, lies off the coast of East Africa. It is the world's fourth largest island. The islands that form the nation of Comoros (below) near Madagascar are oceanic islands that lie over a hot spot region in the Indian Ocean.

There are about 1,190 islands in the Maldives. This aerial view of the Maldives shows just a few of its coral atolls.

Coastlines

The Indian Ocean's coastline is generally fairly smooth. Long stretches of shore are occupied by curving bays and sandy beaches. Beaches take up more than half of India's coastline.

the center of a plate. Over thousands of years, the plume remains in one place while the weak point drifts over it. This can give rise to a group of islands, such as those of Comoros.

High ground meeting the ocean is undercut by waves to form steep cliffs on some coasts, such as those on the Arabian Peninsula and along the coast of southern Australia. Much of the Indian Ocean shore, however, is backed by gently sloping lowlands. Mudflats, sand dunes, and mangrove forests edge the water in many areas. Some of the world's largest **deltas** are located along the coasts of the Indian Ocean. These low-lying regions, home to millions of people, are prone to flooding after heavy rain or storms.

The third type of island is a coral atoll—a hollow ring of coral surrounding a **lagoon** of still water. Examples include the Maldives and outer islands of the Seychelles. Scientists believe these coral **reefs** formed in the shallow waters around volcanic islands that later subsided into the ocean, leaving just the coral ring.

The wide, sandy beaches along the Indian Ocean's shores are popular with vacationers. This beach is on Réunion Island.

The coastlines of the Indian Ocean have a variety of natural features, including sheer cliffs, wide bays, sandy coves, and offshore islands. All these features are shaped by two main processes: erosion and deposition. Erosion is the wearing away of the land by water, wind, and other natural forces. Deposition is the laying down of rocky materials, often in the form of fine particles such as sand, mud, or silt.

Waves are the main force of erosion on coastlines. As they beat against the shore, they hurl sand and **shingle** against rocks to wear them away. Bands of hard rock at the water's edge are left to form jutting headlands, while waves eat away soft rocks to form deep, curving bays. Long stretches of the Indian Ocean's coasts are fringed by coral reefs with sheltered lagoons on their landward sides. The reefs of the Red Sea alone stretch for about 1,240 miles (1,995 km).

Out to sea, the pounding waves smash rocky fragments into sand and shingle. Coastal currents may carry these materials for miles along the shore and then deposit them to form **barrier islands**, beaches, and **spits**. Elsewhere, at river

The towering cliffs along the Great Australian Bight (or bay) on the southern coast of Australia were formed by erosion.

mouths, sediment carried toward the ocean by rivers is dropped to form flat, swampy deltas. The delta of the Indus River is 120 miles (193 km) wide. Many channels cut through the huge, triangular delta of the Ganges River. The channels weave through the enormous amounts of sediment dropped at the river's mouth.

CHAPTER TWO

CLIMATE AND CURRENTS

The Red Sea and the Persian Gulf are among the world's saltiest bodies of water. Their presence in the Indian Ocean increases the ocean's **salinity** level, making it the world's saltiest ocean. Where mighty rivers—such as the Ganges in Asia and the Zambezi and Limpopo in Africa—enter the ocean, however, they produce zones of less salty water.

Water Temperature

Temperatures vary through the ocean depending on the area's **latitude**, season, and water depth. The deepest waters remain very cold all year. The ocean does not extend into cold northern regions,

and so much of the ocean has warm surface temperatures. In the far south, however, the water temperature falls to 30° Fahrenheit (-1° Celsius) in winter. Sometimes, icebergs drift from the Southern Ocean into the southern Indian Ocean.

Monsoon Winds

The monsoon winds north of the **equator** are unusual because they change direction with the seasons, bringing

---

In July 2005, Mumbai, India, came to a standstill when roads were flooded by the monsoon. The rains affected millions of people in the city and surrounding areas.

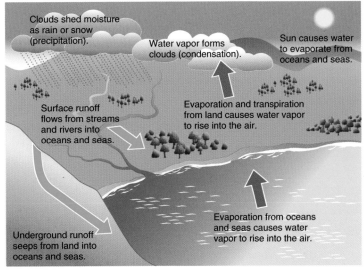

Moisture continually circulates between the oceans, air, and land. This never-ending process, illustrated above, is known as the water cycle.

Clouds shed moisture as rain or snow (precipitation).

Water vapor forms clouds (condensation).

Sun causes water to evaporate from oceans and seas.

Surface runoff flows from streams and rivers into oceans and seas.

Evaporation and transpiration from land causes water vapor to rise into the air.

Underground runoff seeps from land into oceans and seas.

Evaporation from oceans and seas causes water vapor to rise into the air.

heavy monsoon rains at certain times of year. The word *monsoon* comes from the Arabic word for "season." From November to April, dry winds from Northeast Asia blow across India to Africa in the northeast monsoon. From May to October, wet winds blowing across the Indian Ocean during the southwest monsoon bring heavy rains to India. In July 2005, the monsoon brought the heaviest rainfall on record to India's shores near the large city of Mumbai (formerly Bombay), with up to 37 inches (940 millimeters) falling in one day. About one thousand people died in flooding and landslides, and many more were at risk from epidemics of diseases carried by the floodwater.

Currents of the Indian Ocean
The Indian Ocean has a complex pattern of currents. Surface currents are driven by winds blowing across the ocean. In the south, **prevailing winds** cause surface waters to flow round in a vast, counterclockwise **gyre**. The gyre is made up of the South Equatorial, Agulhas, South Indian, and West Australia Currents.

This map shows the main surface currents of the Indian Ocean and reversing currents of the monsoons.

The westward-flowing North Equatorial and the eastward-flowing Equatorial Countercurrent are the main surface currents in the northern part of the ocean. The northern ocean also has surface currents that change direction with the seasonal monsoon winds.

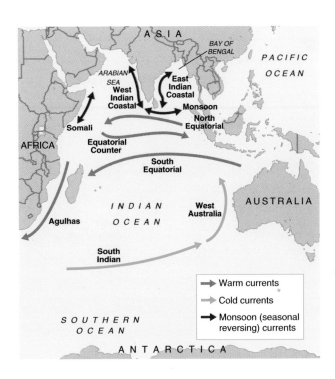

ASIA

BAY OF BENGAL

PACIFIC OCEAN

ARABIAN SEA

West Indian Coastal

East Indian Coastal

Monsoon

North Equatorial

Somali

AFRICA

Equatorial Counter

South Equatorial

INDIAN OCEAN

West Australia

AUSTRALIA

Agulhas

South Indian

SOUTHERN OCEAN

ANTARCTICA

→ Warm currents
→ Cold currents
→ Monsoon (seasonal reversing) currents

What Causes Tides?

Tides are regular rises and falls in sea level caused mainly by the tug of the Moon's gravity. As the Moon orbits Earth, its gravity pulls ocean water into a mound below it. A similar bulge appears on the ocean on the opposite side of Earth because the planet itself is also being pulled, by the same force, away from the water on the far side. As Earth spins eastward, so the mounds move westward across Earth's surface, bringing tides to coasts in succession. Because Earth spins around once every twenty-four hours, the two bulges both move across Earth once in that period, creating two tides a day in each place. The tides are not always equal in volume, however. In some parts of more enclosed seas, such as the Java Sea and Persian Gulf, there is just one tide a day.

The Sun's gravity exerts a similar, but weaker, pull on the oceans. This is because, while many times larger than the Moon, it is also much farther away. Every two weeks, at the full moon and again during the new moon, the Sun and Moon line up so that their pulls combine. This force brings extra high tides called spring tides. They alternate with weaker tides also occurring every two weeks, named neap tides, when the two pulls tend to minimize each other.

As well as surface currents, there are other, deepwater currents in the Indian Ocean, driven by variations in water temperature and salinity. Cold waters—which are rich in nutrients because nutrients mix better with cold waters than with warm waters—rise up seasonally in various places. These cold waters, known as **upwellings**, are found off Somalia, off Oman on the Arabian Peninsula, and south of Java. Upwellings provide excellent feeding grounds for marine life and create good fishing areas.

Sea Levels in the Indian Ocean

The difference in sea levels at high and low tide is called tidal range. On many Indian Ocean coasts, especially in the west, the tidal range is slight. In Chennai (formerly Madras), India, and on the islands of Mauritius and Sri Lanka, tides rise and fall by less than 2 feet (0.6 m). The range is much greater on some eastern shores. On some coasts of Myanmar, spring tides rise and fall by 17 feet (5 m). At Port Hedland in western Australia, the tidal range is 19 feet (5.8 m).

Climate

Climate varies with latitude in the Indian Ocean. Moving north to south, there are several climate zones: the monsoon zone, the trade winds zone, the **subtropical** and **temperate** zones, and the subpolar zone. The monsoon zone and the trade wind zone (between 10° and 30° South) have a **tropical** climate. The subtropical and temperate zones have cooler climates. The subpolar zone in the far south has a harsh climate with strong winds, brief, cool summers, and long, icy winters.

Cyclones

Large tropical cyclones—known as hurricanes in North America—are called severe cyclonic storms in the northern Indian Ocean and tropical cyclones in the southwestern Indian Ocean. Cyclones form in the trade wind belt in late summer and early fall, becoming huge revolving storms that can measure hundreds of miles across and cause enormous damage. They begin far out in the ocean, at centers of **low pressure** where warm, moist air is rising upward. As the rising air cools, its moisture **condenses**, bringing lashing rain and releasing heat that fuels the developing storm. Winds begin to spiral faster and faster around the center of low pressure, which becomes the calm "eye" in the center of the cyclone.

Cyclones often strike tropical and subtropical areas of the Indian Ocean during or just after the monsoon rains. Many cyclones blow themselves out harmlessly in the open ocean, but they can cause great destruction when they sweep ashore, accompanied by high seas. The fierce winds around the cyclone's eye sometimes cause seawater to pile up and form a mound of water called a storm surge, which can hit ocean shores with an impact similar to a tsunami.

Why Is the Ocean Salty?

Ocean water is salty because it contains dissolved minerals, or salts, washed from the land by rivers or released underwater from hydrothermal vents and volcanic eruptions. The salt level in ocean water is higher than in rivers because, when surface water **evaporates**, the dissolved salts remain in the oceans and become more concentrated. The average salt content of the oceans is about 34 parts per thousand. In the Indian Ocean, salt levels vary between 32 parts per thousand (in the Bay of Bengal, for example) and 37 parts per thousand in the Arabian Sea, Red Sea, and Persian Gulf. Experts calculate that the salt in all the seas and oceans would be enough to bury Earth's landmasses to a depth of 500 feet (152 m)! So why don't oceans and seas get increasingly salty as new minerals are added each year? Some salt is removed from the water when it is absorbed by marine life or reacts with underwater rock and eventually forms new sediment layers on the ocean floor. These processes helps keep salt levels constant in the oceans.

The low-lying nation of Bangladesh in Asia has been hit by several major cyclones in recent decades. In 1970, up to 500,000 people died when a

*This **satellite** image shows a tropical cyclone whirling over the Mozambique Channel between Madagascar and the coast of East Africa in 2001.*

powerful cyclone hit the region. In 1991, at least another 200,000 people died in Bangladesh when coasts were swamped by high seas during a large tropical cyclone. In 1998, similar floods made millions homeless in Bangladesh.

Waves and Tsunamis

High winds and storms can whip up towering waves in the Indian Ocean. As waves sweep across the ocean, the water in them moves around in a circle. Out at sea, the water is able to circulate freely, but as they reach the shallow water the waves slow down and rear upward. Their tops spill over to form foaming breakers that crash onto the shore.

Extreme waves called tsunamis can result when an underwater earthquake, volcanic eruption, or landslide disturbs the ocean bed. The waves radiate outward from the center of disturbance like ripples in a pond. Far out in the ocean, these waves are only about 1 foot (30 cm) high and are barely noticeable. They rear up to great heights, however, as they approach land. *Tsunami* is a Japanese word meaning "harbor wave."

Tsunami

"We didn't feel the earthquake here so there was no warning at all. . . . We swam out of the room neck deep in water, forcing our way through the tables and chairs in the restaurant and up into a tree. But within about 30 seconds that tree collapsed as well and we were thrust back into the water where we had to try and keep our heads above the water line. We were swept along for a few hundred meters, trying to dodge the motorcycles, refrigerators, cars and other debris that were coming with us. Finally, about 300 meters inshore, we managed to get hold of a pillar, which we held onto until the waters just gradually began to subside. Other people though weren't so lucky."

Roland Buerk, BBC news reporter, Unawatuna, Sri Lanka, December 26, 2004

The 2004 Tsunamis

On December 26, 2004, a major earthquake and the shocks that followed it sent a series of tsunamis racing across the Indian Ocean at high speed. Effects varied as the waves reached coasts. Some shores were hit by waves up to 50 feet (15 m) high, which washed far inland. Other coasts were struck by a series of smaller surges. On some shores, the water first drained far out to sea and then rushed in again with tremendous force.

The tsunamis traveled up to 3,000 miles (4,800 km), as far as the coasts of Africa. Their effects were greatest in Indonesia and Sri Lanka, where the most people died. In all, eleven nations were badly hit by the tsunamis, which killed between 250,000 and 300,000 people and made millions more homeless. The waves wrecked thousands of miles of coastline and washed right over some islands in the Maldives. The province of Aceh in Sumatra, just east of the earthquake's **epicenter**, was totally devastated, not just by tsunamis but by the quake itself.

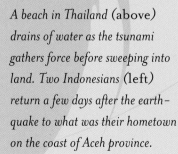

A beach in Thailand (above) drains of water as the tsunami gathers force before sweeping into land. Two Indonesians (left) return a few days after the earthquake to what was their hometown on the coast of Aceh province.

CHAPTER THREE

MARINE LIFE

The Indian Ocean contains a huge variety of marine life, although many species are less abundant here than in other, colder oceans. Some creatures are endemic, which means they are unique to the region. Others are closely related to Pacific or Atlantic species because the Indian Ocean mingles with those waters.

Coastal Habitats

The Indian Ocean has a wide range of coastal **habitats**, including mudflats, salt marshes, beaches, lagoons, and sea cliffs. Mangrove swamps cover long stretches of shoreline including around the mouths of rivers, such as the Indus. Remote islands are home to plant and animal species found nowhere else.

Marine life is abundant around coral reefs, found off the shores of Africa, India, and Myanmar, and in the Persian Gulf and Red Sea. In the eastern ocean, major reefs surround the Andaman, Nicobar, and Chagos Islands. The Indian Ocean has three kinds of reef: fringing reefs that lie just offshore, barrier reefs that form farther out but also run parallel to coasts, and coral atolls.

Life in Shallow Waters

The shallow waters of continental shelves are rich in nutrients carried out to sea by rivers. These nutrients nourish microscopic **algae**, which in turn feed animals of many kinds. Out in the open ocean, nutrients are generally scarce, and marine life is less abundant there than in other oceans. Living things, however, flourish around upwellings off Somalia and in the north Arabian Sea,

The Sundarbans in the Ganges Delta on the coast of India is the world's largest mangrove swamp. Mangrove trees act as nurseries and feeding grounds for hundreds of different species and protect coastal lands during floods.

where cold, mineral-rich water rises up from the depths.

Zones of the Ocean

Scientists divide the waters of the open ocean into vertical layers, each of which forms a separate habitat for marine creatures. Life is most plentiful in the warm, sunlit, upper waters down to 330–660 feet (100–200 m), which are called the euphotic zone. The seaweeds, **plankton**, and other plants that thrive there provide food for creatures including shrimp, jellyfish, and surface-dwelling fish.

In the Ocean Depths

Only faint glimmers of light reach the mid-depths, or **bathyal zone**, between 330–660 feet and 6,600 feet (100–200 m and 2,000 m). Plants cannot thrive in

Coral Reefs

Coral reefs form in warm, shallow waters in the **Tropics** and in subtropical areas. These hard structures are built by small creatures called coral **polyps**. The polyps live in large groups attached to firm surfaces, such as rocks or the reef itself. Like sea anemones, coral animals have tube-shaped bodies with a mouth on top that is surrounded by a ring of tentacles. At night, the polyps spread their tentacles to capture food. They are also fed by tiny algae that live inside them and produce food by **photosynthesis**. The algae are also nourished by the polyp's waste. Natural partnerships such as this are known as symbiosis.

Coral polyps use minerals dissolved in seawater to build a protective, chalky skeleton around their soft bodies. When they die, their cup-shaped skeletons remain and slowly build up on top of others to form a rocky reef. The reefs of the central Indian Ocean include 140

types of coral. In the Red Sea, the reefs are even more diverse, with 350 corals, such as the carnation coral shown above.

the bathyal zone, so animals are also scarce. They are even fewer in the inky-black, ice-cold depths of the **abyssal zone** below 6,600 feet (2,000 m). There, fish survive on scraps of plant and animal food that drift down from above, or they prey on each other.

Flashlight fish, which dwell in the bathyal zone, have light-producing patches below their eyes. By raising or lowering flaps of skin, they can turn these miniature headlights on and off. This helps both to confuse predators and to communicate with others of their species.

Indian Ocean Plant Life

Plant life of the Indian Ocean includes microscopic algae named dinoflagellates. These simple organisms give off tiny

Ocean Food Chains

In the Indian Ocean, as in other oceans, living things depend on one another for food. The relationships between plants and animals in a habitat can be shown in a food chain. Plants form the base of almost all marine food chains. Tiny floating plants, or phytoplankton, and seaweeds use photosynthesis to make their food. Tiny animals called zooplankton, including young fish and shellfish, feed on the plants. They provide food for small fish, such as herrings and sardines, which are

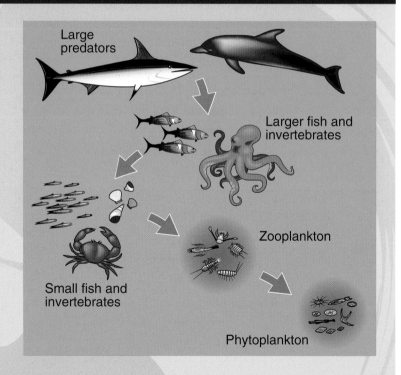

snapped up by larger fish, such as tuna, marlin, and barracudas. In turn, these fish may fall prey to sharks or fishermen. When living things die, their remains are eaten by scavengers and broken down by bacteria, which helps to recycle the energy their bodies contain.

gleams of light that make the sea surface shimmer at night. In coastal shallows and the still waters of lagoons behind coral reefs, sea grasses and seaweeds root. Mangrove trees have long, stilt-like roots that stick out of the mud. Coconut palm trees take root on beaches throughout tropical regions. The fruit of the coco de mer palm in the Seychelles produces the world's largest seed, which weighs up to 48 pounds (22 kilograms). Fruits dropped by coco de mer palms sometimes float away on the ocean, which is why sailors and people on distant shores once believed they were from underwater plants (*mer* is the French word for "sea").

Invertebrates

A high proportion of animals found in the Indian Ocean are invertebrates, or creatures that lack bony inner skeletons. Invertebrates include sponges, **mollusks**, sea urchins, crabs, corals, starfish, and jellyfish. Many of these creatures live attached to the ocean bed, filtering tiny particles of food from the water. Squid, octopus, and cuttlefish—all mollusks—are free swimmers. These animals can shoot jets of water behind them to give themselves a burst of speed. The nautilus is a mollusk with a many-chambered shell. The animal lives in the outer shell chamber; the other cavities are filled with gas, which allow the nautilus to float. The cone shell, a species of marine snail, uses a poisoned dart to prey on other sea snails.

Fish and Reptiles

Vertebrates, or animals with an inner skeleton, include fish, reptiles, birds, and mammals. The Indian Ocean contains thousands of different fish—over four thousand surface dwellers as well as many other species that inhabit the mid-depths and deep ocean.

Seabed dwellers include snapper, bream, skate, and coelacanths. Pelagic species, or surface dwellers, include flying fish that leap out of the water to escape their enemies. These fish can glide up to 1,300 feet (396 m) through the air, propelled by their flickering tails

A male pharaoh cuttlefish guards its mate laying eggs on the floor of the Andaman Sea off the coast of Myanmar.

The Living Fossil

The coelacanth is an ancient fish well known from fossils dating back more than 360 million years. Scientists believed the species had died out millions of years ago. In 1938, however, a living specimen was caught off Comoros, near Madagascar. Some experts say it was the greatest biological find of the century—the coelacanth, known as the "living fossil," provides an extraordinary link to ancient life on Earth. In 1998, a second species of coelacanth was found living off the Indonesian coast. The coelacanth has some unusual features, the most interesting being two pairs of fins that move almost like human arms and legs. Coelacanths grow to about 5–6 feet (1.5–1.8 m) long.

and with their fins outstretched to keep airborne. Fast, predatory fish such as tuna, sailfish, and marlin speed through the open ocean. Sharks and barracudas live in open waters and around coral reefs.

Reptiles of the region include sea snakes and several types of sea turtle, including green, leatherback, hawksbill, and loggerhead turtles. Masirah Island off Oman in the Arabian Sea hosts the world's largest breeding group of loggerhead turtles. Hawksbill and green turtles also nest there. The islands of Aldabra in the Seychelles are home to giant land tortoises. Saltwater crocodiles dwell in the swamps of India and Bangladesh and on the Andaman and Nicobar Islands.

Birds
Albatross glide over the southern seas of the

Seahorses (left) and lionfish (bottom) both live in the Gulf of Aqaba in the Red Sea.

Indian Ocean on huge, outstretched wings. Penguins swim off coasts in the southern islands. In warmer waters, boobies and frigate birds nest in mangrove forests, while tropic birds, shearwaters, and sooty terns breed on remote islands. Shearwaters and terns are among the species that **migrate** long distances. Unique Indian Ocean species include several island birds. The flightless rail, one of the ocean's few surviving flightless birds, lives on Aldabra.

Mammals of the Coasts and Ocean

The Indian Ocean region is home to seals and the dugong, a large, gentle plant eater found in the Persian Gulf, Red Sea, and Australian waters. Also called sea cows, dugongs can live for up to seventy years, but they are now rare because of hunting. The Indian Ocean is a key area for whales, with thirty-three different toothed whales, such as dolphins, porpoises, orcas, and sperm whales. Large whales include humpbacks, fin, blue, and Bryde's whales. Several species of bats live on remote islands —one of the world's largest species, the Livingstone's fruit bat, inhabits the islands of Comoros. Thirty species of lemur live in the forests and swamps of Madagascar. These unusual primates were once also found in mainland Africa but died out there long ago.

A banded sea snake (above) hunts for small fish off the coast of Indonesia. In the far south of the Indian Ocean, king penguins (right) live on the remote Heard Island and in the icy surrounding waters.

CHAPTER FOUR

PEOPLE AND SETTLEMENT

The coasts of East Africa were probably the first part of the Indian Ocean region to be inhabited. Humans began to live there about 100,000 years ago.

Early Migration

From Africa, early people moved north and east into southern Asia, where they inhabited coasts of the Indian Ocean by 60,000 B.C. From eastern Asia, people gradually spread south through Indonesia to reach Australia by 50,000 B.C. Experts believe these first migrations were mainly on foot, using bridges of land that existed between islands at the time because sea levels were lower than they are today.

The Indian Ocean coasts probably attracted people because the seas provided food. People trapped or speared fish in the shallows or gathered shellfish on the shore. The first humans lived a wandering lifestyle, moving from place to place in search of food.

First Farmers

Starting in about 10,000 B.C., farmers began to grow crops and keep livestock in an area known as the Fertile Crescent, which stretches from the eastern part of the Mediterranean Sea to the Persian Gulf. This area probably provides the first example of farming anywhere in the world. By 5000 B.C., farming had spread to Asia. After farming began, people began to settle in one place, and the first villages developed.

Early Civilizations

In ancient times, some of the world's most advanced cultures appeared on or near the coasts of the Indian Ocean. In about 3500 B.C., the civilization of Mesopotamia developed along the Tigris and Euphrates Rivers, which drain into the Persian Gulf. The Mesopotamians were among the first people to irrigate farmland, build cities, and invent a system of writing. From 3000 to 1000 B.C., an Arab civilization named the Dilmun culture flourished on the Arabian Peninsula in what are now Bahrain and eastern Saudi Arabia.

Exploring the Indian Ocean

The Dilmun people and the ancient Egyptians were probably the first people to build boats and explore the ocean's coasts. Dilmun sailors ventured all along

Moroni, capital of Comoros, was a center for Arab merchants who traded in slaves and spices. Many islands and towns along the East African coast still show Arab influence in their architecture and customs.

the coasts of eastern Africa, India, and Southeast Asia. In about 2500 B.C., Egyptians built an irrigation canal across the **isthmus** of Suez to link the Mediterranean Sea with the Red Sea. At high tide, the Egyptians used the canal to gain access to the Indian Ocean, which enabled them to sail south along the African coast. The ancient waterway at Suez remained in use until A.D. 775.

Migration to the Islands

About two thousand years ago, Africans, Arabs, Indians, and Southeast Asians settled some of the Indian Ocean's islands. Madagascar off East Africa, for example, was settled not by Africans, but by people from Indonesia. These seafarers are thought to have crossed the ocean in boats propelled by seasonal winds.

People from India settled Sri Lanka. In the 200s B.C., the islanders converted to the Buddhist religion, while people in India remained mostly Hindu. Buddhists from Sri Lanka then migrated to and settled in the Maldives about A.D. 500.

Trading Networks

From about 2000 B.C. to the late medieval period (approximately A.D. 1300), Arabs dominated trade in the Indian Ocean. The Dilmun and other Arab groups established trading networks that extended right around the coast, from East Africa to Indonesia. Arab ships traded timber and ointments from Africa, rice and cloth from India, dried fish and shells from the Maldives, and spices from Southeast Asia. Through this trading network, and from coastal settlements, Arab culture, scientific knowledge, and religion spread far across the region.

New Arrivals

Arab dominance of the ocean was challenged first by the Chinese and later by

Europeans. During the 1300s, Chinese emperors sent several fleets of large ships called junks to explore the ocean. The Chinese began trading with the peoples of India, the Arabian Peninsula, Africa, and the Maldives. By the late 1400s, Europeans, especially the Portuguese, were building ships capable of long ocean voyages. In 1498, Portuguese explorer Vasco da Gama rounded the tip of South Africa from the Atlantic to become the first European to sail across the Indian Ocean. Other Europeans soon followed. The Portuguese dominated European trade with Asia until the 1600s, when the Netherlands, Britain, Denmark, and France also began to trade.

European Colonies

From the 1500s through the 1700s, European powers claimed as **colonies** many of the lands bordering the Indian Ocean. Britain claimed India, Burma (now Myanmar), Australia, South Africa, and parts of the Arabian Peninsula. Lands in East Africa were divided among

Aboriginal peoples inhabited the region around the city of Perth, Australia, until the British arrived in 1829 and established a colony. The discovery of gold in the 1890s and other valuable metals in the 1960s led to industrialization and growth. Modern Perth (above) is the center for government and business in Western Australia.

the British, Portuguese, Germans, and Italians, while France took control of Madagascar. Much of Southeast Asia was colonized by the Dutch.

European colonization brought many changes to the Indian Ocean. The newcomers began to exploit the resources of the Indian Ocean and its coastal lands for large profits. They set up plantations to grow crops—such as tea, rubber, sugar, and cotton—suited to the hot climate. Coconuts in coastal groves yielded a product called copra, used to make oil and soap. Seabird droppings, or guano, were gathered to use as fertilizer.

Europeans often treated the Native peoples of the Indian Ocean little better than slaves. Native peoples were forced to work long hours in the plantations.

Many thousands died from European diseases that had previously been unknown in the Indian Ocean region.

Early Industrialization

In the 1800s, some colonies became partly industrialized when the first factories making mass-produced goods were built in Asian countries. The Europeans also modernized ports and built railways to speed the export of crops, such as tea from Sri Lanka. Modern industry received a boost when the Suez Canal opened in 1869, speeding trade between Europe, India, and the Far East. In the early 1900s, the discovery of oil in the Persian Gulf brought profits for the British.

Independent Nations

Australia became independent from Britain in 1907. During the 1900s, other colonies along the Indian Ocean won independence from Europe, especially after World War II ended in 1945. When the British left India in 1947, the nation was divided along religious lines between a mainly Hindu India and Muslim-dominated Pakistan. (East Pakistan became Bangladesh in 1971.)

Around the ocean, historic links with Arab, Asian, and European powers live on in the culture, traditions, and religious beliefs of many nations. The people of Indonesia and East Africa, for example, are mainly followers of Islam. European languages are still spoken in

Muslims in Karachi leave a mosque after celebrating the end of the holy month of Ramadan. Karachi was a Hindu trading center from the early 1700s to the mid-1800s. From 1843 to 1947, it was a British possession. Today, Karachi is Pakistan's main port and industrial center and one of the most populated cities in the world.

Mumbai

Mumbai is located on a group of islands on the northwest coast of India. Originally a fishing settlement, this great port lies on a deep bay. Its original name, Bombay, came from the Portuguese term *buan bahia*, meaning "good bay." From the 1660s to 1947, Bombay was controlled by the British. During the 1800s, it grew into a thriving industrial center with a large port. Extensive docks and cotton mills were built following the construction of a railway link with India's cotton-growing region. After India became independent, the city continued to grow as a port, commercial center, and as the home of India's movie industry. With an estimated 18 million inhabitants in the early 2000s, Mumbai is one of the world's most populated urban centers.

several former colonies. Some small islands are still overseas territories of large nations, such as France and Australia, which claimed them long ago.

Growth and Modernization

In the late 1900s, nations of the Indian Ocean, including Indonesia and Thailand, industrialized rapidly. Island nations, such as the Seychelles and Maldives, meanwhile, developed their coastlines in response to mass tourism. The island of Male in the Maldives is home to the nation's capital, also called Male. The town grew from a small port into a modern city in the space of just a few decades. Today, about seventy-five thousand people live there.

Military Importance

Throughout history, the coasts and islands of the Indian Ocean have held strategic importance both for local nations and for distant powers. During colonial times, the English, French, and Dutch set up military bases on Indian

The island of Male in the Maldives, just 1.25 miles (2 km) long, is almost completely covered with buildings.

Ocean islands, including Réunion, Mauritius, and the Seychelles. These bases originally helped combat piracy in the region. Ships could also refuel and take on provisions, and the bases were later used by military aircraft. In times of war, from World War I to the recent war in Iraq, the military bases of the Indian Ocean became even more important. Diego Garcia, the largest of the Chagos Islands, has a strategic position in the middle of the Indian Ocean. All its residents were relocated by Britain between 1965 and 1973, and the island is now a joint U.S.-British military facility.

Ports and Cities

Across the Indian Ocean, ports grew up on coasts and islands where deep bays and inlets created good harbors. Some ports, such as Chennai and Mumbai, date back to before colonial times. Following industrialization and the discovery of oil, cities around large ports expanded rapidly. Factories, oil refineries, and new suburbs sprang up on adjacent shores. Today, large ports include Aden in Yemen, Djibouti (capital of the nation Djibouti), Dar es Salaam in Tanzania, Durban in South Africa, Perth in Australia, and Kolkata in India.

The Vezo people of southwestern Madagascar are often called "the people of the sea." Vezo communities and their traditional way of life are dependent on local fishing. The man in this picture is smoking fish on the beach.

Ways of Life

The shores of the Indian Ocean hold great contrasts in ways of life. Within a few miles of bustling, high-rise cities or large oil terminals are fishing and farming communities where the way of life has changed little for hundreds of years. Whether in ports, towns, or small villages, many coastal people still depend on the sea for their living. They may fish or farm along the coast. They may work in coastal and offshore mines or in the shops, hotels, and restaurants that serve the tourist trade.

Although the ocean provides wealth and employment, it also brings the dangers of cyclones, floods, earthquakes, and tsunamis. Despite these hazards, the coasts of the Indian Ocean in India, Bangladesh, and Indonesia are now densely populated. By population, Karachi in Pakistan and Mumbai in India are two of the world's largest cities.

CHAPTER FIVE

TRANSPORTATION AND COMMUNICATION

A traditional dhow sails along the coast of Zanzibar, off Tanzania in East Africa.

Arab dhows were among the first vessels to sail the Indian Ocean. These graceful, two-masted ships had triangular sails named lateen sails, enabling them to sail into the wind. Arab boat-builders used no nails—instead, timbers were lashed together with coconut fiber.

Vessels of the Indian Ocean

Dhow designs have changed little for centuries, and they still sail the Indian Ocean. There are several other boats seen in the ocean today that have been in use for hundreds—and even thousands—of years. People traveling and fishing along coasts and around islands build small boats of traditional, local design. These vessels include dugout canoes, **outrigger** canoes, catamarans (with two **hulls**), and trimarans (with a main hull and two smaller, balancing hulls).

In medieval times, Chinese junks sailed the open ocean. These huge, wooden ships, up to 180 feet (55 m) long, carried five or six masts with immense, square sails. Below deck, the hull was divided into watertight compartments, which prevented the ship from sinking if it sprang a leak.

Changing Times

In the mid-1800s, fast, narrow sailing ships called clippers began to carry tea across the Indian Ocean. Then steamships appeared, and heavy, steel-hulled vessels replaced wooden ships. Today, traditional small vessels mingle with larger fishing boats, speedboats, and ferries.

Huge **container** ships and oil **tankers** also regularly cross the Indian Ocean.

Beginning in the mid-1900s, airplanes changed the way people traveled across the large distances of the Indian Ocean. Cheap flights began in the 1960s for tourists who wanted to visit Indian Ocean coasts and remote islands. Until the 1970s, the only way to visit islands such as the Seychelles was by boat. After airstrips were built, mass tourism began, and the Seychelles are now a popular vacation destination.

Cargoes of the Indian Ocean

The early dhows and junks traveled the Indian Ocean carrying cargoes of spices, timber, porcelain, and food crops. From the 1500s, European ships carried goods to and from their colonies on Indian Ocean shores. Today, oil is the most valuable cargo that crosses the Indian Ocean. From the Persian Gulf and Indonesia, oil is shipped to Japan and European nations in huge tankers. Large vessels also transport raw materials, including coal and iron ore from India, South Africa, and Australia to Japan and Europe. Manufactured goods generally travel in the opposite direction.

Navigation and Communication

Early Arab sailors developed **navigation** skills well in advance of European sailors. The Arabs used instruments called *kamals*, which could determine latitude by measuring the distance between the horizon and a star. Today, vessels in the Indian Ocean are equipped with a wide range of instruments that show them where they are and help navigate treacherous waters. These instruments include **sonar** and **radar**. Communication systems are essential in the stormy Indian Ocean. Ship-to-shore radios allow ships to maintain regular contact with ports and

Oil tankers line up to fill their tanks with oil at an Iranian loading terminal in the Persian Gulf.

weather stations and obtain up-to-date weather forecasts. Modern compasses and global positioning systems (GPS) help ships pinpoint their positions using satellites. Satellites also provide telephone and Internet communication across the huge distances of the ocean.

At Mahabalipuram, India, where submerged temples were discovered in 2002, the Indian Ocean has yielded another find. The 2004 tsunamis washed away sand to expose what may be an ancient Hindu shrine (above).

Shipping Routes

Before the advent of steamships, sailing ships used variable monsoon winds to speed their voyages back and forth across the Indian Ocean. Today, vessels with diesel, electric, gas, or nuclear-powered engines can travel the busy shipping routes of the ocean at any time of year.

The Indian Ocean has four key channels where shipping is concentrated into narrow bottlenecks: the Bab el Mandeb at the mouth of the Red Sea; the **Strait** of Hormuz at the entrance to the Persian Gulf; the Strait of Malacca, between Indonesia and Malaysia, that leads to the Pacific Ocean; and the Suez Canal.

When the Suez Canal opened in 1869, the ancient Egyptian waterway that once crossed the Suez isthmus had not been in use for more than one thousand years. All ships traveling between the Atlantic and Indian Oceans, therefore, had to go around the southern tip of Africa. The opening of the Suez Canal cut thousands of miles off the journey. The largest supertankers, however, are too big for the canal and must take the long way around.

Indian Ocean Hazards

The Indian Ocean can be a dangerous place for ships. Apart from facing storms and cyclones, vessels can run into sharp reefs, hidden sandbanks, and—in the far south of the ocean—even ice.

The ocean has been notorious for pirates for hundreds of years. Indian, Arab, and European pirates menaced ships in Indian Ocean waters in the

1700s. Piracy was eventually stamped out until, in the 1980s, a new wave of piracy began in Southeast Asia. Modern pirates —traveling in speedboats and equipped with guns and explosives—board ships to steal computers, televisions, and other electronic goods.

Undersea Exploration

Throughout history, ships have been wrecked in the Indian Ocean, including some with precious cargoes. Coastal waters, in particular, hold a number of treasure ships that have been explored in recent years.

Submerged buildings that were once on land have also been explored. In 2002, British and Indian divers uncovered the remains of several ancient temples off Mahabalipuram in southern India.

The first ship to investigate the deep waters of the Indian Ocean was the British research vessel HMS *Challenger*. From 1874 to 1875, *Challenger* cruised the world's oceans, retrieving ocean floor samples and discovering marine animals never seen before. Today, studies of this kind are most often run from the surface, using underwater robots called autonomous underwater vehicles (AUVs) or submersibles named remotely operated vehicles (ROVs). In 2001, U.S. scientists in the research ship *Knorr* used the ROV *Jason* to explore marine life around hydrothermal vents discovered in the Indian Ocean the previous year.

The Ocean Drilling Program

The Integrated Ocean Drilling Program (IODP), set up in 2003, is an international partnership that has grown out of two earlier U.S. programs: the Deep Sea Drilling Project and the Ocean Drilling Program (ODP). The IODP, like its predecessors, explores Earth's formation by drilling into the sediment and rocks that make up the floor of deep ocean basins. In the 1980s, the ODP drilled for many months in the Indian Ocean to investigate how Earth's crust originated. From 1998 to 1999, ODP scientists visited the Kerguelen Plateau in the southern Indian Ocean. They found evidence of ancient volcanoes as well as areas of continental rock that shed new light on the movement of continents millions of years ago.

HMS Challenger *struggles in stormy waters of the southern Indian Ocean off the Kerguelen Islands.*

CHAPTER SIX

RESOURCES

The Indian Ocean's major economic resource is oil. The most productive oil fields are in the Persian Gulf, a 90,000-square-mile (233,000-sq-km) body of water that lies in the northwest part of the Indian Ocean.

A Major Resource

Scientists believe that oil and gas deposits are the remains of marine plants and animals that died millions of years ago and were later buried by layers of sediment on the seabed. Pressure and heat slowly turned the remains to oil and natural gas, which can be extracted and burned to provide a source of energy.

The Indian Ocean only accounts for about 1 percent of the world's natural gas currently being produced. It is rich in deposits of oil, however, and about 40 percent of the world's oil comes from the region. As well as the huge amount of oil extracted from the Persian Gulf, oil is mined in Indian waters—off Mumbai and in the Bay of Bengal—and off the coasts of Indonesia and western Australia. Oil and natural gas have also been located at other sites in the ocean, including in the Arabian Sea and off northern Australia.

Other Mining

Titanium, phosphate, monazite, zircon, and glauconite are among other minerals mined in the Indian Ocean region. The Red Sea is rich in zinc, copper, lead, and manganese. Beach sand in India, Sri Lanka, and Indonesia yields monazite, ilmenite, and other minerals. Thailand and Sumatra have valuable deposits of tin just off their shores. The Aghulas Bank off South Africa is an important source of diamonds. Sand, gravel, and coral are **dredged** from many coastal waters for use in construction.

Far out to sea, the Indian Ocean floor is strewn with mineral deposits named manganese nodules. These lumps contain valuable deposits of iron, nickel, cobalt, and copper as well as manganese. The nodules were discovered in the late 1800s, but no economic way of harvesting the nodules from the deep oceans has yet been devised.

Commercial Fishing

Only about 5 percent of the world's annual fish catch is netted in the Indian Ocean. Fish stocks are smaller there than in either the Pacific or Atlantic Oceans because the warm Indian Ocean waters produce fewer nutrients and therefore support less plankton.

Large, commercial fishing fleets from Japan, South Korea, Russia, and Taiwan operate in the open ocean. Surface-dwelling species, including tuna, are caught by commercial fleets using long lines or purse-seine nets (nets that surround and enclose fish). In coastal waters, anchovies and sardines are trapped in floating gill nets (flat nets that entangle fish) or purse-seine nets. Trawl nets, shaped like giant funnels, are used to catch bottom dwellers, such as snapper and skate. The farming of shellfish, fish,

Oil in the Persian Gulf

A Kuwaiti oil refinery processes oil on the shores of the Persian Gulf.

The Persian Gulf is bordered by the Middle Eastern nations of the United Arab Emirates, Qatar, Saudi Arabia, Kuwait, Iraq, and Iran. The island kingdom of Bahrain is on the western shore of the Gulf. Historically, the Persian Gulf offered rich resources, such as fish, pearls, and coral. In 1908, when the region was under British control, engineers found oil deposits there. Larger finds were made in the 1930s.

Today, more of the world's oil supply comes from the Persian Gulf than from any other region. Since World War II, oil extraction in the Gulf has altered life in bordering nations as well as the local **environment**, but it has also had a global impact. As oil consumption skyrockets, the nations bordering the Persian Gulf have had conflict among themselves and with the rest of the world over the highly valuable resource.

and edible seaweed is also a large industry in the Indian Ocean region, especially on Indonesian coasts.

Farming

The rich soil found on some Indian Ocean coasts and islands is good for growing crops, such as sugarcane, fruits, and flowers. Crops provide food locally, but they are also grown to sell overseas. The economy of the island of Réunion, for example, is based on sugarcane exports. Islands of the Indian Ocean are known for their spices, including cloves

Traditional Fishing in the Indian Ocean

Much of the fishing in the Indian Ocean is done on a small scale. Local fishermen target coastal species—both seabed dwellers, such as snapper and skate, and small fish that swim at the surface, including sardines and anchovies. Around the shores of the Indian Ocean, fishermen still use methods that date back centuries. In regions that have coral reefs, reef-dwelling fish, such as parrotfish and wrasse, may be caught using harpoons and traps. On the coast of Sri Lanka (*top right*), fishermen perch on slender wooden stilts set up in the shallows. In Cochin in eastern India (*bottom right*), nets originally introduced by settlers from China in the thirteenth century can be seen along the shore. In this type, bamboo cages are fitted with tightly woven nets on the bottom. The nets—dipped into and raised from the water by levers—catch fish, squid, and shellfish.

Cloves, one of many spices grown on Indian Ocean islands, are spread out to dry on a quay on the island of Zanzibar (above). Local people depend on tourists to spend money at souvenir markets, such as this one (right) on Mahe Island in the Seychelles.

from Zanzibar in East Africa, cinnamon and vanilla from the Seychelles, and nutmeg and mace from Sri Lanka.

Tourism

Tourism is vital to the economy of many Indian Ocean nations. Every year, millions of vacationers from Europe and elsewhere fly to the region to enjoy the warm, sunny climate, palm-fringed beaches, and varied culture. The region's coral reefs are one of the main attractions. Mass tourism, however, is harming the very reefs that people come to see. In some areas, reefs have been destroyed to make room for new resorts and airports. Tourists and local tradesmen also damage reefs by breaking off pieces of coral for souvenirs.

Tourism is now the mainstay of many island economies, including the Seychelles, the Maldives, and Sri Lanka. These countries can be badly hit if war or natural disaster brings a slump in the tourist trade. Tourist numbers dropped steeply after both the 1991 Gulf War and the 2004 tsunamis, causing hardship for thousands of local tourism workers.

CHAPTER SEVEN

ENVIRONMENT AND THE FUTURE

The Indian Ocean is famed for its clear waters, beautiful scenery, and spectacular wildlife. The rising populations along its coasts and some islands, however, are putting pressure on marine habitats and the wildlife they contain.

Changing Habitats

Huge tracts of forest that once clothed the islands of Madagascar and Mauritius have been felled for logging and to make way for towns and farms. The bare soil left behind washes into the ocean, where it muddies coastal waters and smothers coral reefs. On the coasts of Africa and Indonesia, long stretches of mangroves have been cut to use for wood or to make room for shrimp farms. The construction of resorts on Indian Ocean beaches disrupts the habitats of seabirds and turtles.

Natural disasters, including floods and cyclones, can harm coastal habitats. The 2004 tsunamis wrecked thousands of miles of shoreline, including lagoons, mangrove swamps, and coral reefs.

Air and Land Pollution

Pollution from land is a major hazard in coastal waters. Large cities, such as

Sapphire mining on Madagascar causes deforestation. The island is rapidly losing the hardwoods that make up its rain forests.

Mumbai and Karachi, release untreated **sewage** and chemicals. The sewage, together with agricultural fertilizers running off from farmlands, cause phytoplankton to multiply and smother the ocean surface. Fish, coral polyps, and other marine life suffer as a result. Thousands of tons of pesticides run into the Bay of Bengal and other areas. Paper, sugar, and chemical factories produce poisonous waste that is absorbed by small creatures, such as shrimps, and then passes up the food chain.

Air pollution from India, China, and smaller Asian nations is a serious problem in the Indian Ocean and on its coasts. The burning of **fossil fuels** produces soot, ash, dust, sulfur dioxide, and carbon dioxide that hover in the air over several million square miles of the ocean in a brown haze. The smog causes temperature changes that affect habitats. The harmful chemicals also fall back on ocean and land in the form of acid rain, which causes damage to plant life.

Oil Pollution

The oil industry causes terrible pollution in the Indian Ocean, both near the coasts and out at sea. The Red Sea, the Arabian Sea, and the Persian Gulf are most affected. In those places, oil from rigs and tankers leaks into the Indian Ocean on a daily basis. Significant amounts of oil are deliberately dumped, too, when tankers are washed out at sea. Oil spills caused by occasional shipping accidents

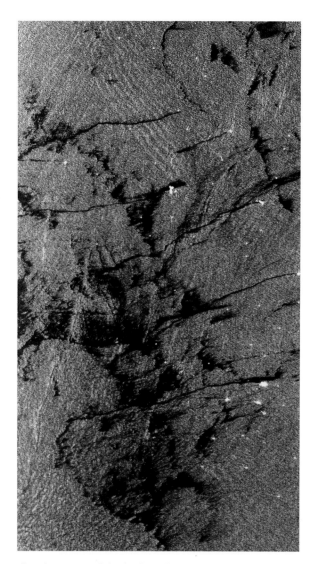

A radar image of the Arabian Sea shows black areas where oil has leaked from offshore oil rigs. The oil has been spread across the sea by wind and currents.

release huge amounts of oil into the ocean. During the 1991 Gulf War, Iraqi forces released several million barrels of oil into the Gulf, killing thousands of fish, seabirds, turtles, and marine mammals. Oil floating in the Indian Ocean also harms the plankton that form the base of marine food chains.

Taking Action

Since the 1980s, nations bordering the ocean—in Africa and Southeast Asia and along the Red Sea and the Persian Gulf—have come together to draft several action plans. In 1994, the Law of the Sea Treaty came into force. This agreement, signed by many Indian Ocean nations, restricts pollution and also controls fishing and mining operations.

A group of sperm whales swims underwater near Sri Lanka. Since the Indian Ocean became a whale sanctuary, stocks of some whale species are starting to recover.

Threatened Species

Overfishing has caused stocks of some fish and shellfish in the Indian Ocean to drop steeply. By the 1960s, whaling had almost brought about the extinction of many types of whales. In 1979, the Indian Ocean was declared a sanctuary for whales.

Seals and dugongs are hunted for their meat, and they also get trapped accidentally in fishing nets. Turtles are killed for their meat, shells, and eggs. In past centuries, hunters wiped out several unique birds. The dodo, a large, flightless bird found only on Mauritius, was hunted to extinction in the 1600s. Another unique island bird, the solitaire, became extinct on its home islands of Réunion and Rodrigues in the 1700s.

Rare island and marine species can be protected by the establishment of marine parks and reserves. These places also safeguard the whole habitat for all plants and animals. The Aldabra Atoll and Vallée de Mai Nature Reserve are both World Heritage Sites in the Seychelles that offer sanctuaries for many endangered species. The flightless rail, one of the Indian Ocean's few surviving flightless birds, lives there, as does the black parrot and threatened birds named red-footed boobies. The sites are also home to the world's largest coco de mer forest, many giant tortoises, and endangered sea turtles.

Early Warning

"The issue of an Indian Ocean early warning system for tsunamis must be urgently addressed. . . . The cost of such a system is likely to be high, but not as high as the suffering of the people affected and the economies of the nations concerned."

Klaus Toepfer, executive director, United Nations Environment Program, 2005

A ring-tailed lemur shares fruit with its young. National parks on Madagascar keep the island's lemurs safe.

The Future of the Indian Ocean

The many millions of people who live on the coastal plains and low-lying islands of the Indian Ocean will face several challenges in the future. A fast-growing population will use more energy, create more waste, and deplete the ocean's resources. The rich oil reserves in the region will not last forever, and new forms of energy will need to be explored. One problem will be a lack of freshwater —ocean water is not drinkable unless the salt has been removed in a process called desalination. Mauritius and the Seychelles are desalinating ocean water, but the process uses a lot of energy. Nuclear power plants combined with desalination plants are now being developed on coasts in India and Pakistan.

As the coastal and island populations grow, more people will be vulnerable to cyclones, earthquakes, and tsunamis than ever before. A tsunami early warning system for the Indian Ocean, installed in 2006, will help avoid disastrous loss of human life in the future.

Global Warming

A climate change identified in the last few years is affecting the world's oceans. World temperatures are slowly but steadily rising, partly because of air pollution from the burning of fossil fuels. Gases given off when these fuels burn trap the Sun's heat to produce warmer weather. The rising temperatures are warming the oceans, which makes the water expand and so raises sea levels. There are signs that land ice in polar regions may melt into the oceans because of warmer temperatures, and this would dramatically raise sea levels. Low-lying countries, such as Bangladesh, could be flooded. Experts think the island nation of the Maldives would be the first to disappear beneath the waves. Warmer water also harms coral reefs. Scientists believe that global warming will also increase the risk of severe weather, including cyclones. Many nations around the world, however, are making an effort to address global warming by reducing energy consumption and cutting down on air pollution.

TIME LINE

About 100,000 B.C. Coast of East Africa is inhabited by early humans.

By 60,000 B.C. People are living on coasts of southern Asia and Southeast Africa.

By 50,000 B.C. People move from eastern Asia to settle Indonesia and Australia.

About 10,000 B.C. Farming begins in Fertile Crescent, a region stretching from the eastern Mediterranean to the Persian Gulf.

About 3500 B.C. Mesopotamian civilization flourishes near Persian Gulf.

About 3000–1000 B.C. Dilmun civilization flourishes on Arabian Peninsula.

About 2500 B.C. Egyptian and Arab sailors begin to travel long distances in Indian Ocean; Egyptians construct irrigation canal across Suez isthmus.

About 2000 B.C. People from Indonesia settle on Madagascar.

About A.D. 500 People from Sri Lanka settle on the Maldives.

1300s Chinese explore Indian Ocean and establish a trading network.

1498 Portuguese explorer Vasco da Gama becomes first European to cross the Indian Ocean.

1500s–1700s European colonial powers claim territories on many Indian Ocean coasts and islands.

By 1681 Dodo of Mauritius becomes extinct.

By 1791 Solitaire of Rodrigues and Réunion Islands becomes extinct.

1869 Suez Canal opens.

1874–1875 British research ship HMS *Challenger* makes the first scientific study of ocean depths, including the Indian Ocean.

1883 Krakatoa eruption causes Indian Ocean tsunamis that kill 36,000 people.

1907 Australia gains independence from Britain.

1908 Oil deposits are found in Persian Gulf.

1938 Coelacanth, believed to be extinct, is found living off the islands of Comoros.

1947 India gains independence and is divided into India and Pakistan.

1970 Powerful cyclone strikes what is now Bangladesh, killing 500,000 people.

1979 Indian Ocean is declared a whale sanctuary.

1991 Several million barrels of oil are released into Persian Gulf during Gulf War; floods caused by cyclone kill more than 200,000 people in Bangladesh.

1994 Law of the Sea Treaty comes into effect.

2000 Japanese scientists discover hydrothermal vents in Indian Ocean.

2001 Hydrothermal vents are explored by ROV *Jason*.

2004 Tsunamis caused by ocean earthquake off Indonesia devastate northeastern coasts of Indian Ocean and part of African coast.

2005 March: Another severe earthquake strikes off Indonesia.

July: Mumbai, India, is hit by heaviest monsoon rains ever recorded.

GLOSSARY

abyssal zone ocean below 6,600 feet (2,000 m)

algae tiny, simple plants or plant-like organisms that grow in water or damp places

barrier island island lying parallel to the shore that protects mainland from the open ocean

bathyal zone mid-depths of ocean water between 330–660 feet deep and 6,600 feet deep (100–200 m deep and 2,000 m deep)

colony territory claimed by a nation or area occupied by settlers

condense change from gas into liquid

container large crate—used on ships, trains, and trucks—that combines many smaller pieces of freight into one shipment for efficient loading and unloading by crane

continental drift theory that landmasses are not fixed but slowly drift across Earth's surface because of tectonic plate movement

current regular flow of water in a certain direction

delta land composed of mud and sand deposited around the mouth of a river

dredge gather by scooping up or digging out

environment surrounding conditions in which living things exist

epicenter point from which the shock waves of an earthquake appear to start

equator imaginary line around the middle of Earth lying an equal distance between the North Pole and South Pole

euphotic zone upper layer of ocean water, usually defined as above 330–660 feet (100–200 m)

evaporate change from liquid into gas

fossil fuel coal, oil, natural gas, and other fuels formed in the ground from remains of plants or animals

gulf large inlet of an ocean

gyre surface current in an ocean or sea that moves in a clockwise or counterclockwise circle

habitat type of place, such as a mountain or coral reef, where plants and animals live

hot spot weak point in Earth's crust where magma breaks through a gradually moving tectonic plate

hull body of a ship. Some vessels have two hulls, joined by a deck or other structure, for stability.

isthmus narrow strip of land connecting two larger landmasses

lagoon shallow area of water near a larger body of water

latitude distance north or south of the equator

low pressure atmospheric system that produces unstable, stormy weather. (High air pressure produces stable weather with clear skies.) Air pressure is the weight of the atmosphere pressing down on Earth at any given point.

magma molten rock beneath the surface of Earth

mantle part of Earth between the crust and core. It is mostly solid rock, but part of it is molten.

migrate move from one place to another

mineral natural, non-living substance

mollusk group of animals with thin, sometimes soft shells, including clams, octopuses, squid, and snails

navigation use of animal instinct or scientific skills to determine a route or steer a course on a journey

outrigger framework attached to the side of a canoe to support a float that gives the boat stability

overfishing catching so many fish that stocks are depleted or species made extinct

peninsula piece of land jutting out into water but connected to mainland

photosynthesis process in which plants use carbon dioxide, hydrogen, and light to produce their food

plankton microscopic plants (phytoplankton) and animals (zooplankton) that float at the surface of oceans and lakes and provide food for many larger animals

polyp small sea animal with tube-like body and tentacles that attaches to rock or other substance

prevailing wind main wind in a particular region

radar system that detects and locates objects by bouncing radio waves off them

reef chain of rock or coral or raised strip of sand in water

Richter Scale scale used to express the power of earthquakes. Very severe earthquakes measure more than seven. No recorded earthquake has measured more than ten.

ridge raised area on land or on ocean bottom

salinity level of salt in water

satellite vehicle that orbits Earth that can be used to send signals to Earth for communications systems; or any object in space that orbits another, larger object

sediment loose particles of rocky material, such as sand or mud

sewage dirty water from homes and factories containing chemicals and human waste

shingle deposit of small rocks, like large gravel, usually found on coastlines

sonar (short for sound navigation and ranging) system that uses sound waves to measure ocean depth and detect and locate underwater objects

spit long, narrow finger of land stretching out into water

strait water channel that connects two areas of water

subduction zone region where two tectonic plates press together, causing one to subduct, or dive below the other

submarine fan area where mud and sand deposited by a river has built up on the seabed. It is similar to a delta, but it is underwater.

submersible small underwater craft often used to explore deep parts of the ocean

subtropical in or having to do with the region of the world that borders the Tropics

tanker ship fitted with tanks for carrying liquid

temperate in or having to do with the regions of the world that lie between the Tropics and the polar regions

tropical in or having to do with the region of the world known as the Tropics

Tropics region of the world either side of the equator between the tropic of Cancer and the tropic of Capricorn

tsunami giant ocean wave caused by underwater earthquake, landslide, or volcanic eruption

upwelling periodic rise of dense, cold water to the ocean's surface when warmer surface waters are pulled away by currents

FURTHER RESOURCES

Books

Hoyt, Erich. *Whale Rescue: Changing the Future for Endangered Wildlife.* Firefly Animal Rescue (series). Firefly Books, 2005.

Innes, Brian. *Down to a Sunless Sea: The Strange World of Hydrothermal Vents.* Sagebrush, 2000.

Oleksy, Walter. *Mapping the Seas.* Watts Library—Geography (series). Franklin Watts, 2002.

Rhodes, Mary Jo. *Sea Turtles.* Undersea Encounters (series). Children's Press, 2005.

Taylor, Leighton. *The Indian Ocean.* Life in the Sea (series). Blackbirch Press, 1998.

Torres, John A. *Disaster in the Indian Ocean: Tsunami 2004.* Monumental Milestones: Great Events of Modern Times (series). Mitchell Lane Publishers, 2005.

Vogel, Carole Garbuny. *Savage Waters.* The Restless Sea (series). Franklin Watts, 2003.

Woodward, John. *Twilight Zone.* Exploring the Oceans (series). Heinemann, 2004.

Web Sites

JASON—Lost City Hydrothermal Vents—Kids' Corner
lostcity.jason.org/kids_corner.aspx

Reef Education Network
www.reef.edu.au/

Savage Earth: Waves of Destruction
www.pbs.org/wnet/savageearth/tsunami/index.html

USGS Earthquake Hazards Program—For Kids Only
earthquake.usgs.gov/4kids/

What's the Story on Oil Spills?
response.restoration.noaa.gov/kids/spills.html

WWF Habitats Home
www.panda.org/news_facts/education/middle_school/habitats/index.cfm

About the Author

Jen Green worked in publishing for fifteen years. She is now a full-time author and has written more than 150 books for children about natural history, geography, the environment, history, and other topics.

INDEX